And earth will call her flowers

To hasten out of doors,—

By their curtsies and

sweet=smelling,

To give grace to my fortelling.

A LAY OF THE EARLY ROSE.

Through the Year

with

Mrs. Browning

I am content to be so weak,—
Put strength into the words I speak,
And I am strong in what I seek.
            A Vision   Poets.

Boston
DeWolfe, Fiske & Co.

TYPOGRAPHY AND PRESSWORK BY
S. J. PARKHILL & CO.
BOSTON, U. S. A.

Through the Year with

Mrs. Browning

January 1

The face of all the world is changed, I think,
Since first I heard the footsteps of thy soul
Move still, O still, beside me as they stole
Betwixt me and the dreadful outer brink
Of obvious death, where I, who thought to sink
Was caught up into love, and taught the whole
Of life in a new rhythm.

Sonnets from the Portuguese.

January 2

Said a people to a poet — ' Go out from
  among us straightway !
  While we are thinking earthly things,
  thou singest of divine.
There's a little fair brown nightingale, who,
  sitting in the gateway,
  Makes fitter music to our ear than any
  song of thine !'

The Poet and the Bird.

January 3

And love! earth's love! and *can* we love
Fixedly where all things move?
    Can the sinning love each other?
      Mother, mother,
I tremble in thy close embrace —
I feel thy tears adown my face —
    Thy prayers do keep me out of bliss —
    O dreary earthly love!

                Isobel's Child.

January 4

She was 'ware of a shadow that crossed
    where she lay;
She was 'ware of a presence that withered
    the day; —
Wild she sprang to her feet, — 'I surrender
    to *thee*
The broken vow's pledge, the accursed rosarie.
    I am ready for dying!'
        The Lay of the Brown Rosary.

January 5

Speak low to me, my Saviour, low and sweet
From out the hallelujahs, sweet and low,
Lest I should fear and fall, and miss Thee so,
Who art not missed by any that entreat.

                Comfort.

January 6

Eve is a twofold mystery —
    The stillness Earth doth keep ;
The motion wherewith human souls
    Toward each other leap !
As if all spirits, which Earth inherits,
    Foreknew they part in sleep.

The Poet's Vow.

January 7

What ! dost thou judge it a strange thing,
That poets, crowned for conquering,
Should bear some dust from out the ring ?

. . . .

And no one looking round the wood
Could help confessing, as he stood,
This Poet-God is glad and good !

A Vision of Poets.

January 8

'Tis well ! I would not doom thy years
Of golden prime, to only tears.
Fair girl ! 'twere better than thine eyes
Should find a joy in summer skies,
As if their sun were on thy fate.
Be happy ; strive not to be great ;
And go not, from thy kind apart,
With lofty soul and stricken heart.

To a Poet's Child.

January 9

Let none say, God preserve the Queen! —
   but rather, Bless the bride! —
None blow the trump, none bend the knee,
   none violate the dream
Wherein no monarch, but a wife, she to her-
   self may seem!
Or if ye say, Preserve the Queen! — oh,
   breathe it inward low.

Crowned and Wedded.

January 10

Far out, kindled by each other,
   Shining hills on hills arise ;
Close as brother leans to brother
   When they press beneath the eyes
Of some father praying blessings from the
   gifts of Paradise.

The Lost Bower.

January 11

'Yes!' I answered you last night ;
   'No!' this morning, Sir, I say !
Colours seen by candle-light,
   Will not look the same by day.

The Lady's 'Yes.'

January 12

Ask the old why they weep, and not the
　　children,
　　　　For the outside earth is cold,—
And we young ones stand without, in our
　　bewildering,
　　　　And the graves are for the old!
　　　　　　　The Cry of the Children.

January 13

Bind, bind the wreath! the slender ring
　　Thy wedded fingers press!
May he who calls thy love his own,
　　Call so thine happiness!

　　　　To Victoire on her Marriage.

January 14

Ever, evermore the while in a slow silence
　　she kept smiling,—
　　And approached him slowly, slowly, in a
　　　　gliding measured pace;
With her two white hands extended as if
　　praying one offended,
　　And a look of supplication, gazing earnest
　　　　in his face.
　　　　　　Lady Geraldine's Courtship.

January 15

Some respect to social fictions
  Hath been also lost by me;
And some generous genuflexions,
  Which my spirit offered free
To the pleasant old conventions of our false
    Humanity.

The Lost Bower.

January 16

I will paint her as I see her!
  Ten times have the lilies blown
  Since she looked upon the sun.

And her face is lily-clear —
  Lily-shaped, and dropped in duty
  To the law of its own beauty.

A Portrait.

January 17

I am renewed:
My eyes grow with the light which is in thine;
The silence of my heart is full of sound.
Hold me up — so! Because I comprehend
This human love, I shall not be afraid
Of any human death; and yet because
I know this strength of love, I seem to know
Death's strength, by that same sign.

A Drama of Exile.

January 18

A knight of gallant deeds,
  And a young page at his side,
From the holy war in Palestine
  Did slow and thoughtful ride,—
As each were a palmer, and told for beads
  The dews of the eventide.

The Romaunt of the Page.

January 19

Calm the stars and golden,
  In a light exceeding:
What their rays have measured
  Let your hearts fulfil!
These are stars beholden
  By your eyes in Eden;
Yet, across the desert,
  See them shining still.

A Drama of Exile.

January 20

I would build a cloudy House
  For my thoughts to live in;
When for earth too fancy-loose,
  And too low for Heaven.
Hush! I talk my dream aloud—
  I build it bright to see,—
Build it on the moonlit cloud,
  To which I looked with *thee.*

The House of Clouds.

January 21

I loved thee — for the Babel curse
    Was meant not for the heart:
I parted from thee, in such way
    As those who love may part.
And now a change hath come to us,
    A sea doth rush between!
I do not know if we can be
    Again as we have been.
             To Victoire on her Marriage.

January 22

Because it was not well, it was not well,
Nor tuneful with thy lofty-chanted part
Among the Oceanides,— that Heart
To bind and bare, and vex with vulture fell.
I would, my noble England! men might seek
All crimson stains upon thy breast — not
    cheek!

             Crowned and Buried.

January 23

'The poet died last month; and nòw
The world, which had been somewhat slow
In honouring his living brow,

'Commands the palms — they must be strown
On his new marble very soon,
In a procession of the town.'

             A Vision of Poets.

January 24

Experience, like a pale musician, holds
A dulcimer of patience in his hand ;
Whence harmonies we cannot understand,
Of God's will in His worlds, the strain un-
    folds
In sad perplexed minors.

> *Perplexed Music.*

January 25

Said he,— ' Wake me by no gesture,— sound
    of breath, or stir of vesture ;
  Let the blessèd apparition melt not yet to
    its divine !
No approaching — hush, no breathing ! or
    my heart must swoon to death in
  The too utter life thou bringest,— O thou
    dream of Geraldine ! '

> *Lady Geraldine's Courtship.*

January 26

A vocal pathos rolls ! and He who drew
All life from dust, and for all, tasted death,
By death and life and love, appealing, saith,
Do you think of Me as I think of you?

> *L. E. L.'s Last Question*

January 27

And wept the page, and laughed the knight,—
  A careless laugh laughed he :
'Well done it were for thy sistèr,
  But not for my ladyè !
My love, so please you, shall requite
No woman, whether dark or bright,
  Unwomaned if she be.'

The Romaunt of the Page.

January 28

Of all the thoughts of God that are
Borne inward unto souls afar,
Along the Psalmist's music deep,
Now tell me if that any is,
For gift or grace, surpassing this —
'He giveth His belovèd sleep'?

The Sleep.

January 29

All my losses did I tell you,
  Ye, perchance, would look away;—
Ye would answer me, 'Farewell ! you
  Make sad company to-day ;
And your tears are falling faster than the
  bitter words you say.'

The Lost Bower.

January 30

And low on his body she droppeth adown —
'Didst call me thine own wife, beloved —
    thine own?
Then take thine own with thee! thy coldness
    is warm
To the world's cold without thee! Come,
    keep me from harm
      In a calm of thy teaching!'
        The Lay of the Brown Rosary.

January 31

I think we are too ready with complaint
In this fair world of God's.   Had we no hope
Indeed beyond the zenith and the slope
Of yon grey blank of sky, we might be faint
To muse upon eternity's constraint
Round our aspirant souls.   But since the scope
Must widen early, is it well to droop,
For a few days consumed in loss and taint?

      Cheerfulness taught by Reason.

February 1

A poet could not sleep aright,
For his soul kept up too much light
Under his eyelids for the night:

And thus he rose disquieted,
With sweet rhymes ringing through his head,
And in the forest wandered.

A Vision of Poets.

February 2

There's a lady — an earl's daughter; she is
  proud and she is noble;
  And she treads the crimson carpet, and she
  breathes the perfumed air;
And a kingly blood sends glances up her
  princely eye to trouble,
  And the shadow of a monarch's crown is
  softened in her hair.

Lady Geraldine's Courtship.

February 3

'His sweetest friend, or hardest foe,
  Best angel, or worst devil;
I either hate or — love him so,
  I can't be merely civil!'

Amy's Cruelty.

February 4

Learn to win a lady's faith
    Nobly, as the thing is high ;
Bravely, as for life and death,—
    With a loyal gravity.
Lead her from the festive boards,
    Point her to the starry skies ;
Guard her, by your truthful words,
    Pure from courtship's flatteries.

The Lady's ' Yes.'

February 5

Yet I could not choose but love her : I was
    born to poet-uses,
    To love all things set above me, all of good
    and all of fair.
Nymphs of old Parnassus mountain, we are
    wont to call the Muses ;
    And in silver-footed climbing, poets pass
    from mount to star.

Lady Geraldine's Courtship.

February 6

Eve.   There is pity in Thee,
O sinned against, great God ! — My seed,
    my seed,
There is hope set on Thee — I cry to Thee,
Thou mystic seed that shalt be ! — leave us
    not
In agony beyond what we can bear.

A Drama of Exile.

February 7

And five hundred archers tall did besiege the
    castle wall,—
And the castle, seethed in blood, fourteen
    days and nights had stood,
        And to-night, anears its fall.
           Rhyme of the Duchess May.

February 8

I am near thee, and I love thee!
Were I loveless, from thee gone,
Love still is round, beneath, above thee —
God, the omnipresent One.
Spread the wing, and lift the brow —
Well-beloved, what fearest thou?
           The Seraphim.

February 9

Our thoughts grow blank, our words grow
    strange;
    We cheer the pale gold-diggers —
Each soul is worth so much on 'Change,
    And marked, like sheep, with figures.
          Be pitiful, O God!
           The Cry of the Human.

I will paint her

as I see her!

Ten times have

the lilies blown

Since she looked upon the sun.

A Portrait.

February 10

Weep, as if you thought of laughter!
Smile, as tears were coming after!
Marry your pleasures to your woes;
And think life's green well worth its rose!

Song.

February 11

I was only a poor poet, made for singing at
    her casement,
   As the finches or the thrushes, while she
      thought of other things.
Oh, she walked so high above me, she ap-
      peared to my abasement,
   In her lovely silken murmur, like an angel
      clad in wings!

Lady Geraldine's Courtship.

February 12

They look up with their pale and sunken faces,
         And their looks are sad to see,
For the man's grief abhorrent draws and presses
         Down the cheeks of infancy —
'Your old earth,' they say, 'is very dreary;
    Our young feet,' they say, 'are very weak!
Few paces have we taken, yet are weary —
    Our grave-rest is very far to seek!'

The Cry of the Children.

February 13

Haply it is angels' duty,
    During slumber, shade by shade
To fine down this childish beauty
    To the thing it must be made,
Ere the world shall bring it praises, or the
    tomb shall see it fade.

A Child Asleep.

February 14

' He will kiss me on the mouth
Then, and lead me as a lover,
    Through the crowds that praise his deeds !
    And, when soul-tied by one troth,
Unto *him* I will discover
    That swan's nest among the reeds.'

The Romance of the Swan's Nest.

February 15

I have lost — oh, many a pleasure —
    Many a hope, and many a power —
Studious health and merry leisure —
    The first dew on the first flower !
But the first of all my losses was the losing
    of the bower.

The Lost Bower.

February 16

Jesus, Victim, comprehending
    Love's divine self-abnegation,
Cleanse my love in its self-spending,
    And absorb the poor libation!
Wind my thread of life up higher,
Up through angels' hands of fire!
I aspire while I expire!
                    Bertha in the Lane.

February 17

We murmur, — 'Where is any certain tune
Or measured music, in such notes as these?'
But angels, leaning from the golden seat,
Are not so minded! their fine ear hath won
The issue of completed cadences;
And, smiling down the stars, they whisper —
    Sweet.

                    Perplexed Music.

February 18

But since to him when living,
    Thou wert both sun and moon,
Look o'er his grave, surviving,
    From a high sphere alone
Sustain that exaltation —
    Expand that tender light;
And hold in mother-passion
    Thy Blessed in thy sight.
                    A Mournful Mother.

February 19

'A nun in the east wall was buried alive,
Who mocked at the priest when he called her
  to shrive, —
And shrieked such a curse as the stone took
  her breath,
The old abbess fell backward and swooned
  unto death
   With an Ave half-spoken.'
    The Lay of the Brown Rosary.

February 20

Vision unto vision calleth,
 While the young child dreameth on,
Fair, O dreamer, thee befalleth
 With the glory thou hast won!
Darker wert thou in the garden, yestermorn,
 by summer sun.

    A Child Asleep.

February 21

   Mother of the world,
Take heart before this Presence. Rise, aspire
Unto the calms and magnanimities,
The lofty uses, and the noble ends,
The sanctified devotion and full work,
To which thou art elect for evermore,
First woman, wife, and mother.

    A Drama of Exile.

February 22

' A rose that droppeth from the hand, that
    fadeth in the breast, —
Until, in grieving for the worst, we learn what
    is the best!'
Then breaking into tears, — ' Dear God,' she
    cried, 'and must we see
All blissful things depart from us, or ere we
    go to Thee?'
The Lay of the Brown Rosary.

February 23

And while the poet seemed to tread
Along the drowsy noise so made,
The forest heaved up overhead

Its billowy foliage through the air,
And the calm stars did, far and fair,
O'erswim the masses everywhere.
A Vision of Poets.

February 24

Then she smiled around right childly, then
    she gazed around right queenly,
And I bowed — I could not answer.   Al-
    ternated light and gloom —
While as one who quells the lions, with a
    steady eye serenely,
She, with level fronting eyelids, passed out
    stately from the room.
Lady Geraldine's Courtship.

February 25

I will look out to his future —
 I will bless it till it shine!
Should he ever be a suitor
 Unto sweeter eyes than mine,
  Sunshine gild them,
  Angels shield them,
Whatsoever eyes terrene
Be the sweetest HIS have seen!

 Catarina to Camöens.

February 26

Then the boy wept aloud; 'twas a fair sight,
 yet sad
To see the tears run down the sweet blooms
 he had:
He stamped with his foot, said — ' The saints
 know I lied,
Because truth that is wicked is fittest to hide!
 Must I utter it, mother?'

 The Lay of the Brown Rosary.

February 27

' Give smoother answers, lying page,
 Or perish in the lying.' —
' I trow that if the warrior brand
Beside my foot were in my hand,
 'Twere better at replying.'
They cursed her deep, they smote her low,
They cleft her golden ringlets through:
 The Loving is the Dying.

 The Romaunt of the Page.

February 28

Hark! the flow of the four rivers —
  Hark the flow!
How the silence round you shivers,
  While our voices through it go
Cold and clear.

A Drama of Exile.

February 29

                    God keeps a niche
In Heaven to hold our idols! and albeit
He brake them to our faces, and denied
That our close kisses should impair their
    white, —
I know we shall behold them raised com-
    plete, —
The dust shook from their beauty, — glori-
    fied
New Memnons singing in the great God-light.

Futurity.

March 1

'Sit still upon your thrones,
  O ye poetic ones!
And if, sooth, the world decry you,
Let it pass unchallenged by you.

A Lay of the Early Rose.

March 2

Two sayings of the Holy Scriptures beat
Like pulses, in the Church's brow and breast;
  .   .   .   .
One is, AND JESUS WEPT, — whereon is prest
Full many a sobbing face that drops its best
And sweetest waters on the record sweet: —
And one is where the Christ, denied and scorned,
LOOKED UPON PETER! *The Two Sayings.*

March 3

And this I meant to say,
  My lady's face shall shine
As ladies' faces use, to greet
  My page from Palestine:
Or, speak she fair, or prank she gay,
  She is no lady of mine.

The Romaunt of the Page.

March 4

He fell before the Angel's feet,
Saying — 'If what is true is sweet,
In something I may compass it.

'For, where my worthiness is poor,
My will stands richly at the door,
To pay shortcomings evermore.'
A Vision of Poets.

March 5

Now Christ bless you with the one light
Which goes shining night and day!
May the flowers which grow in sunlight,
Shed their fragrance in your way!

Wine of Cyprus.

March 6

Eve. Shall I be mother of the coming life?
Hear the steep generations, how they fall
Adown the visionary stairs of Time,
Like supernatural thunders — far, yet near;
Sowing their fiery echoes through the hills.
Am I a cloud to these — mother to these?
  Earth Spirits. And bringer of the curse
    upon all these.
A Drama of Exile.

March 7

Here she paused, — she had been paler at
　　the first word of her speaking ;
　But because a silence followed it, blushed
　　scarlet, as for shame ;
Then, as scorning her own feeling, resumed
　　calmly — ' I am seeking
　More distinction than these gentlemen
　　think worthy of my claim.'

Lady Geraldine's Courtship.

March 8

Lucifer.　Now may all fruits be pleasant
　　to thy lips,
Beautiful Eve !　The times have somewhat
　　changed
Since thou and I had talk beneath a tree ;
Albeit ye are not gods yet.

A Drama of Exile.

March 9

' Dear neighbour of the trellised house,
　　A man should murmur never,
Though treated worse than dog and mouse
　　Till doted on forever.'

Amy's Cruelty.

March 10

'And so he died,' I whispered. — 'Nay,
Not *so*,' the childish voice did say —
'That Poet turned him, first, to pray

In silence ; and God heard the rest,
''Twixt the sun's footsteps down the west.
Then he called one who loved him best.'

A Vision of Poets.

March 11

'O young page,' said the knight,
    'A noble page art thou !
Thou fearest not to steep in blood
    The curls upon thy brow ;
And once in the tent, and twice in the fight,
    Didst ward me a mortal blow.'

The Romaunt of the Page.

March 12

By grace of God ! his face is stern,
As one compelled, in spite of scorn,
To teach a truth he could not learn.

A Vision of Poets.

March 13

By hours of night, — that when the air
　Its dew and shadow yields,
We still may hear the voice of God
　In silence of the fields.
Oh! then sleep comes on us like death,
　All soundless, deaf, and deep:
Lord! teach us so to watch and pray,
　That death may come like sleep.

Hymn.

March 14

Fix not thy sight, so long and fast
　Upon the shroud's despair;
Look upward unto Zion's hill,
　For death was also *there!*
And think, ' The death, the scourge, the scorn,
　My sinless Saviour bore —
The curse — the pang, too deep for tears —
　That *I* should weep no more!'

Remonstrance.

March 15

And the poets wander, said I,
　Over places all as rude!
Bold Rinaldo's lovely lady
　Sate to meet him in a wood —
Rosalinda, like a fountain, laughed out pure
　with solitude.

The Lost Bower.

March 16

But ah!—alas for her!
No thing did minister
To her praises, to her praises,
More than might unto a daisy's.

A Lay of the Early Rose.

March 17

Jesus, victim, comprehending
Love's divine self-abnegation,
Cleanse my love in its self-spending,
And absorb the poor libation!
Wind my thread of life up higher—
Up through angels' hands of fire!—
I aspire while I expire!

Bertha in the Lane.

March 18

There is a land of rest deferred:
Nor eye hath seen, nor ear hath heard,
Nor Hope hath trod the precinct o'er;
For hope beheld is hope no more!
There, human pulse forgets its tone—
There, hearts may know as they are known!
Oh, for dove's wings, thou dwelling blest,
To fly to *thee*, and be at rest!

Weariness.

March 19

'Ten nightingales shall flee
  Their woods for love of me, —
Singing sadly all the suntide,
  Never waiting for the moontide.'

A Lay of the Early Rose.

March 20

'What right *can* you have, God's other works,
    to scorn, despise, . . . revile them
  In the gross, as mere men, broadly — not
    as *noble* men, forsooth, —
But as Pariahs of the outer world, forbidden
    to assoil them,
  In the hope of living — dying, — near that
    sweetness of your mouth?'

Lady Geraldine's Courtship.

March 21

'When death shrouds thy memory,
  Love is no shrine —
The dear eyes that weep for thee,
  Soon sleep like thine!
The wail murmured over thee,
  Fainteth away;
And the heart which kept love for thee,
  Turns into clay!'

The Vision of Fame.

March 22

'Tis a morn for a bridal; the merry bride-bell
Rings clear through the greenwood that skirts
  the chapelle;
And the priest at the altar awaiteth the bride,
And the sacristans slyly are jesting aside
   At the work shall be doing.
    The Lay of the Brown Rosary.

March 23

Henceforward, human eyes of lovers be
The only sweetest sight that I shall see,
With tears between the looks raised up to me.

     A Drama of Exile.

March 24

The old Earl he smiled smooth, then he sighed
  for wilful youth, —
'Good my niece, that hand withal looketh
  somewhat soft and small,
   For so large a will, in sooth.'
    Rhyme of the Duchess May.

March 25

I have been in the meadows all the day,
And gathered there the nosegay that you see;
Singing within myself as bird or bee
When such do field-work on the morn of May:
But now I look upon my flowers, — decay
Has met them in my hands, more fatally,
Because more warmly clasped, — and sobs are
    free
To come instead of songs.   *Irreparableness.*

March 26

O the little birds sang east, and the little birds
    sang west, —
O and laughed the Duchess May, and her
    soul did put away
        All his boasting for a jest.
            Rhyme of the Duchess May.

March 27

Then the sword he leant upon, shivered —
    snapped upon the stone.
'Sword,' he thought, with inward laugh, 'ill
    thou servest for a staff,
        When thy nobler use is done!'
            Rhyme of the Duchess May.

March 28

I, reigning the earth's empress, yesterday,
Put off from me, to-day, your hate with prayers!
I, yesterday, who answered the Lord God,
Composed and glad, as singing-birds the sun,
Might shriek now from our dismal desert,
   'God;'
And hear Him make reply, 'What is thy need,
Thou whom I cursed to-day?'

       A Drama of Exile.

March 29

Her hair was tawny with gold, her eyes with
    purple were dark,
Her cheeks pale opal burnt with a red and
    restless spark.

       A Court Lady.

March 30

But her brother had passed in between them
    and her,
And calmly knelt down on the high altar stair—
Of an infantile aspect so stern to the view,
That the priest could not smile on the child's
    eyes of blue,
    As he would for another.

       The Lay of the Brown Rosary.

March 31

Be satisfied ;
Something thou hast to bear through woman-
    hood —
Peculiar suffering answering to the sin ;
Some pang paid down for each new human life;
Some weariness in guarding such a life —
Some coldness from the guarded; some mistrust
From those thou hast too well served ; from
    those beloved
Too loyally some treason.

A Drama of Exile.

April 1

'And earth will call her flowers
  To hasten out of doors, —
By their curtsies and sweet-smelling,
To give grace to my foretelling.

A Lay of the Early Rose.

April 2

'Get thee in, thou soft ladye! here is never
  a place for thee!
'Braid thine hair and clasp thy gown, that
  thy beauty in its moan
    May find grace with Leigh of Leigh.'

Rhyme of the Duchess May.

April 3

God, there is power in Thee! I make
    appeal
Unto Thy kingship.

A Drama of Exile.

April 4

She felt the scimitar gleam down,
    And met it from beneath,
With smile more bright in victory
    Than any sword from sheath, —
Which flashed across her lip serene,
Most like the spirit-light between
    The darks of life and death.

The Romaunt of the Page.

April 5

                'Tis a human heart,
And so confesses, with a human fear ; —
That only for the hope the cross inspires,
That only for the MAN who died and lives,
'Twould crouch beneath thy sceptre's royalty,
With faintness of the pulse, and backward
        cling
To life.   *A Seaside Meditation.*

April 6

' And this I meant to fear, —
    Her bower may suit thee ill !
For, sooth, in that same field and tent,
    Thy *talk* was somewhat still ;
And fitter thine hand for my knightly spear
    Than thy tongue for my lady's will.'

The Romaunt of the Page.

April 7

Napoleon ! he hath come again — borne home
Upon the popular ebbing heart, — a sea
Which gathers its own wrecks perpetually,
Majestically moaning.   Give him room ! —
Room for the dead in Paris ! welcome solemn
And grave deep, 'neath the cannon-moulded
     column !   *Crowned and Buried.*

April 8

The maidens looked forward, the youths
    looked around,
The bridegroom's eye flashed from his prayer
    at the sound ;
And each saw the bride, as if no bride she were,
Gazing cold at the priest without gesture of
    prayer,
      As he read from the psalter.
     The Lay of the Brown Rosary.

April 9

  ' Now hearken ! ' Then the poet gazed
  Upon the angel glorious-faced,
  Whose hand, majestically raised,

  Floated across the organ-keys,
  Like a pale moon o'er murmuring seas,
  With no touch but with influences.

       A Vision of Poets.

April 10

Then from out her bower chambère did the
    Duchess May repair, —
'Tell me now what is your need,' said the
    lady, 'of this steed,
        That ye goad him up the stair?'
           Rhyme of the Duchess May.

April 11

Many vassals bow before her, as her chariot
    sweeps their doorways;
  She hath blest her little children, — as a
    priest or queen were she!
Oh, too tender or too cruel far her smile upon
    the poor was,
  For I thought it was the same smile which
    she used to smile on *me*.
        Lady Geraldine's Courtship.

April 12

It was thus I reeled! I told you that her
    hand had many suitors —
  But she rose above them, smiling down, as
    Venus down the waves, —
And with such a gracious coldness, that they
    could not press their futures
  On that present of her courtesy, which
    yieldingly enslaves.
        Lady Geraldine's Courtship.

April 13

Angel and organ, and the round
Of spirits, solemnised and crowned, —
While the freed clouds of incense wound

Ascending, following in their track,
And glimmering faintly, like the rack
O' the moon, in her own light cast back.
A Vision of Poets.

April 14

For we sometimes gently wrangled;
    Very gently, be it said, —
For our thoughts were disentangled
    By no breaking of the thread!
And I charged you with extortions
    On the nobler fames of old —
Ay, and sometimes thought your Porsons
    Stained the purple they would fold.
Wine of Cyprus.

April 15

' " The stars walk statelier round the edge
O' the silver spheres, and give in pledge
Their light for nobler privilege." '

A Vision of Poets.

April 16

'It is three months gone to-day since I gave
    mine hand away.
Bring the gold and bring the gem, we will
    keep bride-state in them,
        While we keep the foe at bay.'
                    Rhyme of the Duchess May.

April 17

Rose-trees, either side the door, were
    Growing lithe and growing tall;
Each one set a summer warder
    For the keeping of the hall, —
With a red rose, and a white rose, leaning,
    nodding at the wall.
                    The Lost Bower.

April 18

We overstate the ills of life, and take
Imagination, given us to bring down
The choirs of singing angels overshone
By God's clear glory, down our earth to rake
The dismal snows instead, flake following flake,
To cover all the corn.   We walk upon
The shadow of hills across a level thrown,
And pant like climbers.   *Exaggeration.*

April 19

Learn more reverence, Madam, not for rank
  or wealth *that* needs no learning ;
   That comes quickly — quick as sin does !
   ay, and often works to sin ;
But for Adam's seed, MAN ! Trust me, 'tis a
  clay above your scorning,
   With God's image stamped upon it, and
   God's kindling breath within.
         Lady Geraldine's Courtship.

April 20

World's use is cold — world's love is vain, —
World's cruelty is bitter bane ;
But pain is not the fruit of pain.

         A Vision of Poets.

April 21

Why, what right have you, made fair by that
  same God — the sweetest woman
   Of all women He has fashioned — with
   your lovely spirit-face,
Which would seem too near to vanish, if its
  smile were not so human, —
   And your voice of holy sweetness, turning
   common words to grace.
         Lady Geraldine's Courtship.

April 22

Thus I thought of the old singers,
   And took courage from their song,
Till my little struggling fingers
   Tore asunder gyve and thong
Of the lichens which entrapped me, and the
   barrier branches strong.

The Lost Bower.

April 23

'I came, I knelt beside her bed;
   Her calm was worse than strife.
"My husband, for thy father dear,
   Gave freely when thou wert not here
   His own and eke my life.
A boon! Of that sweet child we make
An orphan for thy father's sake,
   Make thou, for ours, a wife."'

The Romaunt of the Page.

April 24

O love, my love! I felt him near again!
I saw his steed on mountain-head, I heard it
   on the plain!
Was this no weal for me to feel?—is
   greater weal than this?
Yet when he came I wept his name—and the
   angels heard but *his*.

The Lay of the Brown Rosary.

April 25

But a three months' joyaunce lay 'twixt that
  moment and to-day, —
When five hundred archers tall stand beside
  the castle wall,
  To recapture Duchess May.
  Rhyme of the Duchess May.

April 26

Patiently enduring,
  Painfully surrounded,
Listen how we love you —
  Hope the uttermost —
Waiting for that curing
  Which exalts the wounded,
Hear us sing above you —
  EXILED, BUT NOT LOST !
  A Drama of Exile.

April 27

The linden-tree that covers thee, might so
  have shadowed twain, —
For death itself I did not fear — 'tis love
  that makes the pain.
Love feareth death ! I was no child — I was
  betrothed that day ;
I wore a troth-kiss on my lips, I could not
  give away !
  The Lay of the Brown Rosary.

April 28

'But no!' say the children, weeping faster,
  'He is speechless as a stone!
And they tell us, of His image is the master
  Who commands us to work on.'

        The Cry of the Children.

April 29

Could ye bless him, father — mother,
  Bless the dimple in his cheek?
Dare ye look at one another
  And the benediction speak?
Would ye not break out in weeping and con-
  fess yourselves too weak?

        A Child Asleep.

April 30

Shapes of brightness overlean thee,
  With their diadems of youth
Striking on thy ringlets sheenly, —
  While thou smilest, . . . not in sooth
Thy smile . . . but the overfair one, dropt
  from some æthereal mouth.

        A Child Asleep.

May 1

'As it is — your ermined pride, I swear, shall
  feel this stain upon her —
That *I*, poor, weak, tost with passion,
  scorned by me and you again,
Love you, Madam — dare to love you — to
  my grief and your dishonour,
To my endless desolation, and your impo-
  tent disdain!'
  Lady Geraldine's Courtship.

May 2

'Quite low-born, self-educated! somewhat
  gifted though by nature,
And we make a point of asking him, — of
  being very kind.
You may speak, he does not hear you! and
  besides, he writes no satire,
These new charmers keep their serpents
  with the antique sting resigned.'
  Lady Geraldine's Courtship.

May 3

Not a step the wood advances
  O'er the open hill-top's bound:
There, in green arrest, the branches
  See their image on the ground:
You may walk beneath them smiling, glad
  with sight and glad with sound.
  The Lost Bower.

May 4

What a day it was, that day!
Hills and vales did openly
Seem to heave and throb away,
At the sight of the great sky;
And the silence, as it stood
In the glory's golden flood,
Audibly did bud and bud!

Bertha in the Lane.

May 5

Help me, God — help me, man! I am low, I
am weak —
Death loosens my sinews and creeps in my
veins;
My body is cleft by these wedges of pains.

Rhapsody of Life's Progress.

May 6

High and low the serfs looked out, red the
flambeaus tossed about, —
From the courtyard rose the cry — 'Live the
Duchess and Sir Guy!'
But she never heard them shout.

Rhyme of the Duchess May.

May 7

Oh, say not it is vain to weep
   That deafened bier above;
When genius has made room for death,
   And life is past from love;
That tears can never his bright looks
   And tender words restore:
I know it is most vain to weep—
   And therefore weep the more!

Remonstrance.

May 8

The Saviour looked on Peter. Ay, no word—
No gesture of reproach! The Heavens serene,
Though heavy with armed justice, did not lean
Their thunders that way! The forsaken Lord
Looked only on the traitor.

The Look.

May 9

Since without Thee we do no good,
   And with Thee do no ill,
Abide with us in weal and woe,—
   In action and in will.

Hymn.

May 10

Have patience, O dead father mine! I did not
    fear to die; —
I wish I were a young dead child and had thy
    company!
I wish I lay beside thy feet, a buried three-
    year child,
And wearing only a kiss of thine upon my
    lips that smiled!
The Lay of the Brown Rosary.

May 11

Truth is fair: should we forego it?
Can we sigh right for a wrong!
God Himself is the best Poet,
And the Real is His song.
Sing His truth out fair and full,
And secure His beautiful
        Let Pan be dead.
          The Dead Pan.

May 12

Hang up my harp again —
    I have no voice for song!
Not song but wail, and mourners pale,
    Not bards, to love belong!
O failing human love!
    O light by darkness known!
O false, the while thou treadest earth!
    O deaf beneath the stone!
      Margret, Margret.   *Margret.*

May the flowers which grow

in sunlight

Shed their fragrance in your way!

MRS. BROWNING.

May 13

'Have you any answer, Madam? If my spirit
    were less earthy—
  If its instrument were gifted with more vi-
    brant silver strings—
I would kneel down where I stand, and say—
    Behold me! I am worthy
Of thy loving, for I love thee! I am worthy
    as a king.'

          Lady Geraldine's Courtship.

May 14

Speak not! he is consecrated—
    Breathe no breath across his eyes;
Lifted up and separated,
    On the hand of God he lies
In a sweetness beyond touching, held in clois-
  tral sanctities.

          A Child Asleep.

May 15

Then the young lord jerked his breath, and
    sware thickly in his teeth,—
'He would wed his own betrothed, an she
    loved him an she loathed,
    Let the life come or the death.'

          Rhyme of the Duchess May.

May 16

'For oh,' say the children, 'we are weary,
　　And we cannot run or leap ;
If we cared for any meadows, it were merely
　　To drop down in them and sleep.'

　　　　　　　The Cry of the Children.

May 17

Thank God, bless God, all ye who suffer not
More grief than ye can weep for.　That is
　　well—
That is light grieving ! lighter, none befell
Since Adam forfeited the primal lot.

　　　　　　　　　　　　Tears.

May 18

'Something, it is, to hold,
　　In God's worlds manifold,
First revealed to creature-duty,
Some new form of His mild Beauty ! '

　　　　　　A Lay of the Early Rose.

May 19

I do not praise this man : the man was flawed
For Adam — much more, Christ ! — his knee
    unbent,
His hand unclean, his aspiration pent
Within a sword-sweep — pshaw ! — but since
    he had
The genius to be loved, why, let him have
The justice to be honoured in his grave.

            Crowned and Buried.

May 20

Do ye hear the children weeping and disprov-
    ing,
    O my brothers, what ye preach ?
For God's possible is taught by His world's
    loving —
    And the children doubt of each.

        The Cry of the Children.

May 21

' Look up — there is a small bright cloud
    Alone amid the skies !
So high, so pure, and so apart,
    A woman's glory lies.'
The page looked up — the cloud was sheen —
A sadder cloud did rush, I ween,
    Betwixt it and his eyes.

        The Romaunt of the Page.

May 22

Oh, the world is weak.
The effluence of each is false to all ;
And what we best conceive, we fail to speak.
Wait, soul, until thine ashen garments fall !
And then resume thy broken strains, and seek
Fit peroration, without let or thrall.

Insufficiency.

May 23

' Earl Walter was a brave old earl, —
 He was my father's friend ;
And while I rode the lists at court,
 And little guessed the end, —
My noble father in his shroud,
Against a slanderer lying loud,
 He rose up to defend.'

The Romaunt of the Page.

May 24

' Five true friends lie for my sake in the moat
 and in the brake, —
Thirteen warriors lie at rest, with a black
 wound in the breast,
 And none of these will wake.'

Rhyme of the Duchess May.

May 25

But now before her people's face she bendeth
    hers anew,
And calls them, while she vows, to be her
    witness thereunto.
She vowed to rule, and in that oath, her
    childhood put away —
She doth maintain her womanhood, in vow-
    ing love to-day.

Crowned and Wedded.

May 26

' Bring the charge, prove the charge, brother !
    speak it aloud —
Let thy father and hers hear it deep in his
    shroud ! '
— ' O father, thou seest, for dead eyes can see,
How she wears on her bosom a *brown rosarie*,
    O my father beloved ! '

The Lay of the Brown Rosary.

May 27

We linger, we linger,
    The last of the throng !
Like the tones of a singer
    Who loves his own song.

A Drama of Exile.

May 28

And the ivy, veined and glossy,
　　Was inwrought with eglantine;
And the wild hop fibred closely,
　　And the large-leaved columbine,
Arch of door and window-mullion, did right
　　sylvanly entwine.

The Lost Bower.

May 29

She was patient with my talking; and I loved
　　her — loved her certes,
　　As I loved all heavenly objects, with uplifted
　　eyes and hands!
As I loved pure inspirations — loved the
　　graces, loved the virtues, —
　　In a Love content with writing his own
　　name on desert sands.

Lady Geraldine's Courtship.

May 30

' A boon, thou noble knight,
　　If ever I servèd thee!
Though thou art a knight and I am a page,
　　Now grant a boon to me;
And tell me sooth, if dark or bright,
If little loved or loved aright,
　　Be the face of thy ladye.'

The Romaunt of the Page.

May 31

If all the gentlest-hearted friends I know
Concentred in one heart their gentleness,
That still grew gentler, till its pulse was less
For life than pity, — I should yet be slow
To bring my own heart nakedly below
The palm of such a friend, that he should
    press
Motive, condition, means, appliances,
My false ideal joy and fickle woe,
Out full to light and knowledge.

                An Apprehension.

June 1

'What glory then for me
In such a company? —
Roses plenty, roses plenty,
And one nightingale for twenty!'

The Lay of the Early Rose.

June 2

And if they asked for rights, he made reply,
'Ye have my glory!'—and so, drawing
round them
His ample purple, glorified and bound them
In an embrace that seemed identity.
He ruled them like a tyrant — true! but none
Were ruled like slaves! Each felt Napoleon!

Crowned and Buried.

June 3

'O dreary life,' we cry, 'O dreary life!'
And still the generations of the birds
Sing through our sighing, and the flocks and
herds
Serenely live while we are keeping strife
With Heaven's true purpose in us, as a knife
Against which we may struggle!

Patience taught by Nature.

June 10

Have I not been nigh a mother
 To thy sweetness, — tell me, dear?
Have we not loved one another
 Tenderly, from year to year,
Since our dying mother mild
Said with accents undefiled,
' Child be mother to this child!'
    Bertha in the Lane.

June 11

Low she dropt her head, and lower, till her
 hair coiled on the floor, —
And tear after tear you heard, fall distinct as
 any word
  Which you might be listening for.
   Rhyme of the Duchess May.

June 12

Mine ears were deaf to melody,
 My lips were dumb to sound:
Where didst thou wander, oh my soul,
 When ear and tongue were bound?
' I wandered by the stream of time,
 Made dark by human tears:
I threw my voice upon the waves,
 And *they* did throw me theirs.'
   A Vision of Life and Death.

June 13

The sovran angel lifted high
His hand, and spake out sovranly —
'Tried poets, hearken and reply!'

A Vision of Poets.

June 14

Albeit, as some have done,
Ye grope tear-blinded, in a desert place,
And touch but tombs, — look up! Those
tears will run
Soon, in long rivers, down the lifted face,
And leave the vision clear for stars and sun.

Tears.

June 15

'Ne'ertheless, you see, I seek it — not because I am a woman,' —
(Here her smiles sprang like a fountain,
and, so, overflowed her mouth)
'But because my woods in Sussex have some
purple shades at gloaming,
Which are worthy of a king in state, or
poet in his youth.'

Lady Geraldine's Courtship.

June 16

I curse you both,

Adam and Eve! Say grace as after meat,
After my curses. May your tears fall hot
On all the hissing scorns o' the creatures here,
And yet rejoice. Increase and multiply,
Ye and your generations, in all plagues,
Corruptions, melancholies, poverties,
And hideous forms of life and fears of death.

A Drama of Exile.

June 17

Face to face with the true mountains,
  I stood silently and still;
Drawing strength for fancy's dauntings,
  From the air about the hill,
And from Nature's open mercies, and most
  debonair goodwill.

The Lost Bower.

June 18

'And if we labour, it shall be
As suiteth best with our degree,
In after-dinner reverie.'

A Vision of Poets.

June 19

What aileth the bridegroom?   He glares
  blank and wide —
Then suddenly turning, he kisseth the bride —
His lip stung her with cold : she glanced up-
  wardly mute :
'Mine own wife,' he said, and fell stark at
  her foot
      In the word he was saying.
              The Lay of the Brown Rosary.

June 20

By your truth she shall be true,
    Ever true, as wives of yore ; —
And her *Yes*, once said to you,
    SHALL be Yes for evermore.

              The Lady's ' Yes.'

June 21

Eve.   *I*, at last,
Who yesterday was helpmate and delight
Unto mine Adam, am to-day the grief
And curse-mete for him !

              A Drama of Exile.

June 22

Memory's the streamlet of the scene
Which sweeps the hills of Life between;
And, when our walking hour is past,
Upon its shore we rest at last;
And love to view the waters fair,
And see lost joys depictured there.

Memory.

June 23

Mine eyes are weary of surveying
The fairest things too soon decaying;
Mine ears are weary of receiving
The kindest words — ah, past believing!
Weary my hope, of ebb and flow;
Weary my pulse, of tunes of woe.

Weariness.

June 24

The wreath which lay on shrine that day, at
vespers bloomed no more —
The woman fair who placed it there had died
an hour before!
Both perished mute, for lack of root, earth's
nourishment to reach; —
O reader, breathe (the ballad saith) some
sweetness out of each!

The Lay of the Brown Rosary.

June 25

'But my lover will not prize
All the glory that he rides in,
   When he gazes in my face.
He will say, " O Love, thine eyes
Build the shrine my soul abides in,
   And I kneel here for thy grace!"'

The Romance of the Swan's Nest.

June 26

Twice he wrung her hands in twain; but the
   small hands closed again, —
Back he reined the steed — back, back! but
   she trailed along his track,
   With a frantic clasp and strain!

Rhyme of the Duchess May.

June 27

Thy hand which plucked the apple, I clasp
   close;
Thy lips which spake wrong counsel, I kiss
   close, —
I bless thee in the name of Paradise,
And by the memory of Edenic joys
Forfeit and lost.

A Drama of Exile.

The essence of

all beauty

I call Love.

A DRAMA OF EXILE.

June 28

And passing homeward through the wood,
He prayed along the solitude,
'Thou, Poet-God, art great and good!

'And though we must have, and have had
Right reason to be earthly sad,
Thou, Poet-God, art great and glad.'
A Vision of Poets.

June 29

I saw alone, dim, white, and grand,
As in a dream, the angel's hand
Stretched forth in gesture of command,

Straight through the haze — And so, as erst,
A strain, more noble than the first,
Mused in the organ, and outburst.
A Vision of Poets.

June 30

And her custom was to praise me when I
    said, — ' The Age culls simples,
    With a broad clown's back turned broadly,
      to the glory of the stars —
We are gods by our own reck'ning, — and
    may well shut up the temples,
    And wield on, amid the incense-steam, the
      thunder of our cars.'
Lady Geraldine's Courtship.

July 1

I looked upward and beheld her! With a
    calm and regnant spirit,
    Slowly round she swept her eyelids, and
      said clear before them all —
'Have you such superfluous honour, sir, that,
    able to confer it,
    You will come down, Mr. Bertram, as my
      guest to Wycombe Hall?'

Lady Geraldine's Courtship.

July 2

'O brave knight,' said the page,
  'Or ere we hither came,
We talked in tent, we talked in field,
  Of the bloody battle-game:
But here, below this greenwood bough,
  I cannot speak the same.'

The Romaunt of the Page.

July 3

Eagles may view thy face — clouds can as-
    suage
Thy fiery wrath — the sage
Can mete thy stature — thou shalt fade with
    age,
Thou art not like to God.

The Image of God.

July 4

And they praised me in her presence ; —
   'Will your book appear this summer ?'
Then returning to each other — 'Yes, our
   plans are for the moors.'
Then with whisper dropped behind me —
   'There he is ! the latest comer,
Oh, she only likes his verses ! what is over,
   she endures.'

Lady Geraldine's Courtship.

July 5

Napoleon ! — 'twas a high name lifted high :
It met at last God's thunder, sent to clear
Our compassing and covering atmosphere,
And open a clear sight beyond the sky
Of supreme empire ; this of earth's was done,
And kings crept out again to feel the sun.

Crowned and Buried.

July 6

'Twas a Duke's fair orphan-girl, and her
   uncle's ward, the Earl,
Who betrothed her twelve years old, for the
   sake of dowry gold,
     To his son Lord Leigh, the churl.

Rhyme of the Duchess May.

July 7

No strength, no need! Then, soul of mine,
  Look up and triumph rather —
Lo! in the depth of God's Divine,
  The Son adjures the Father —
          BE PITIFUL, O GOD!
          The Cry of the Human.

July 8
  ' Nay, let me in,' said she,
  ' Before the rest are free, —
In my loneness, in my loneness,
All the fairer for that oneness.
  ' For I would lonely stand
  Uplifting my white hand,
On a mission, on a mission,
To declare the coming vision.'
          A Lay of the Early Rose.

July 9

There is one hill I see nearer,
  In my vision of the rest;
And a little wood seems clearer,
  As it climbeth from the west,
Sideway from the tree-locked valley, to the
  airy upland crest.
          The Lost Bower.

July 10

Cripples once danced i' the vines — and bards
    approved,
    Were once by scornings moved!
But love strikes one hour — LOVE. Those
    never loved,
    Who dream that they loved ONCE.
Loved Once.

July 11

They have lifted him up, — but his head
    sinks away, —
And his face showeth bleak in the sunshine,
    and grey.
Leave him now where he lieth — for oh,
    never more
Will he kneel at an altar or stand on a floor!
    Let his bride gaze upon him!
The Lay of the Brown Rosary.

July 12

And a stranger when he sees her
    In the street even, smileth stilly,
    Just as you would at a lily.

And all voices that address her
    Soften, sleeken, every word,
    As if speaking to a bird.
A Portrait.

July 13

With the sense accursed and instant, that if
    even I spake wisely
  I spake basely — using truth, if what I
    spake indeed was true,
To avenge wrong on a woman — *her*, who
    sate there weighing nicely
  A poor manhood's worth, found guilty of
    such deeds as I could do!
               Lady Geraldine's Courtship.

July 14

And if Chaucer had not travelled
  Through a forest by a well,
He had never dreamt nor marvelled
  At those ladies fair and fell,
Who lived smiling without loving, in their
  island citadel.
               The Lost Bower.

July 15

Truth is large.   Our aspiration
Scarce embraces half we be.
Shame! to stand in his creation
And doubt Truth's sufficiency! —
To think God's song unexcelling
The poor tales of our own telling —
        When Pan is dead.
            The Dead Pan.

July 16

Alone, amid the shifting scene,
That central altar stood serene
In its clear steadfast taper-sheen.

Then first, the poet was aware
Of a chief angel standing there
Before that altar, in the glare.
A Vision of Poets.

July 17

'Go to!' say the children — 'up in Heaven,
  Dark, wheel-like, turning clouds are all we
    find!
Do not mock us; grief has made us unbeliev-
    ing —
  We look up for God, but tears have made
    us blind.'
The Cry of the Children.

July 18

'Accept me therefore — Not for price,
  And not for pride, my sacrifice
  Is tendered! for my soul is nice,

'And will beat down those dusty seeds
  Of bearded corn if he succeeds
  In soaring while the covey feeds.'
A Vision of Poets.

July 19

Farewell! — a word that human lips bestow
On all that human hearts delight to know :
On summer skies, and scenes that change as
    fast ;
On ocean calms, and faith as fit to last ;
On Life, from Love's own arms, that breaks
    away ;
On hopes that blind, and glories that decay !

To the Memory of Sir Uvedale Price, Bart.

July 20

Here a linden-tree stood, brightening
    All adown its silver rind ;
For as some trees draw the lightning,
    So this tree, unto my mind,
Drew to earth the blessed sunshine, from the
    sky where it was shrined.

          The Lost Bower.

July 21

We should see the spirits ringing
    Round thee, — were the clouds away !
'Tis the child-heart draws them, singing
    In the silent-seeming clay —
Singing! — Stars that seem the mutest go in
    music all the way.

          A Child Asleep.

July 22

Quote he, ' Get thee from this strife, — and
  the sweet saints bless thy life ! —
In this hour, I stand in need of my noble
  red-roan steed —
    But not of my noble wife.'

Rhyme of the Duchess May.

July 23

The next pool they came near unto
Was bare of trees: there, only grew
Straight flags and lilies fair to view,

Which sullen on the water sate,
And leant their faces on the flat,
As weary of the starlight-state.

A Vision of Poets.

July 24

' And now He pleadeth up in heaven
  For our humanities,
Till the ruddy light on seraph's wings
  In pale emotion dies.
They can better bear His Godhead's glare
  Than the pathos of His eyes !'

The Poet's Vow.

July 25

But at last there came a pause.   I stood all
  vibrating with thunder,
Which my soul had used.   The silence drew
  her face up like a call.
Could you guess what word she uttered? She
  looked up as if in wonder,
With tears beaded on her lashes, and said,
  'Bertram!' it was all.

Lady Geraldine's Courtship.

July 26

Mortal man and woman,
    Go upon your travel!
Heaven assist the Human
    Smoothly to unravel
All that web of pain
    Wherein ye are holden.

A Drama of Exile.

July 27

'I ween the very skies
  Will look down with surprise,
When low on earth they see me,
With my starry aspect dreamy!'

A Lay of the Early Rose.

July 28

Oh, a bride of queenly eyes, with a front of
    constancies, —
Oh, a bride of cordial mouth, — where the
    untired smile of youth
      Did light outward its own sighs.

Rhyme of the Duchess May.

July 29

Put the broidery-frame away,
    For my sewing is all done !
The last thread is used to-day,
    And I need not join it on.
    Though the clock stands at the noon,
    I am weary !   I have sewn,
    Sweet, for thee a wedding-gown.

Bertha in the Lane.

July 30

Ever, evermore the while in a slow silence
    she kept smiling,
    But the tears ran over lightly from her
    eyes, and tenderly : —
' Dost thou, Bertram, truly love me ? Is no
    woman far above me,
    Found more worthy of thy poet-heart than
    such a one as I ? '

Lady Geraldine's Courtship.

July 31

'True,' say the children, 'it may happen
  That we die before our time :
Little Alice died last year, her grave is shapen
  Like a snowball, in the rime.
We looked into the pit prepared to take her :
 Was no room for any work in the close clay !
From the sleep wherein she lieth none will
  wake her,
  Crying, "Get up, little Alice ! it is day." '
       The Cry of the Children.

August 1

O earth, so full of dreary noise!
O men, with wailing in your voice!
O delvèd gold that wailers reap!
O strife, O curse, that o'er it fall!
God strikes a silence through you all,
And 'giveth His belovèd sleep.'

The Sleep.

August 2

Half-ashamed and half-softened, the boy did
    not speak,
And the blush met the lashes which fell on
    his cheek:
She bowed down to kiss him — Dear saints,
    did he see
Or feel on her bosom the BROWN ROSARIE —
    That he shrank away weeping?
The Lay of the Brown Rosary.

August 3

Softened, quickened to adore her, on his knee
    he fell before her —
    And she whispered low in triumph — 'It
    shall be as I have sworn!
Very rich he is in virtues, — very noble —
    noble, certes;
    And I shall not blush in knowing that men
    call him lowly born!'
Lady Geraldine's Courtship.

August 4

In that ancient hall of Wycombe, thronged
  the numerous guests invited,
  And the lovely London ladies trod the
  floors with gliding feet;
And their voices low with fashion, not with
  feeling, softly freighted
  All the air about the windows, with elastic
  laughters sweet.

Lady Geraldine's Courtship.

August 5

No flowers our gardened England hath,
To match with these in bloom and breath,
  Which from the world are hiding
In sunny Devon moist with rills, —
A nunnery of cloistered hills, —
  The elements presiding.

A Flower in a Letter.

August 6

'Dost thou fear?' he said at last: 'Nay,' she
  answered him in haste, —
'Not such death as we could find — only life
  with one behind.
  Ride on fast as fear, ride fast!'

Rhyme of the Duchess May.

August 7

I tell you, hopeless grief is passionless —
That only men incredulous of despair,
Half-taught in anguish, through the midnight
    air
Beat upward to God's throne in loud access
Of shrieking and reproach.   Full desertness
In souls, as countries, lieth silent-bare
Under the blenching, vertical eye-glare
Of the absolute Heavens.   *Grief.*

August 8

There be none of England's daughters who
    can show a prouder presence ;
  Upon princely suitors suing she has looked
    in her disdain :
She was sprung of English nobles, I was born
    of English peasants ;
  What was *I* that I should love her — save
    for feeling of the pain ?

        Lady Geraldine's Courtship.

August 9

    ' Holy in voice and heart, —
      To high ends set apart !
  All unmated, all unmated,
  Because so consecrated ! '

      A Lay of the Early Rose.

August 10

The page stopped weeping, and smiled cold—
' Your wisdom may declare
That womanhood is proved the best
By golden brooch and glossy vest
    The mincing ladies wear:
Yet is it proved, and was of old,
Anear as well — I dare to hold —
By truth, or by despair.'

The Romaunt of the Page.

August 11

A paleness took the poet's cheek :
' Must I drink *here?* ' he questioned meek
The lady's will, with utterance weak.

' Ay, ay,' she said, ' it so must be,'—
(And this time she spake cheerfully),
' Behoves thee know world's cruelty.'

A Vision of Poets.

August 12

Small the wood is, green with hazels,
    And, completing the ascent,
Where the wind blows and sun dazzles,
    Thrills in leafy tremblement :
Like a heart that, after climbing, beateth
quickly through content.

The Lost Bower.

August 13

And God knows, who sees us twain,
   Child at childish leisure,
I am near as tired of pain
   As you seem of pleasure ; —
Very soon too, by His grace
   Gently wrapt around me,
Shall I show as calm a face,
   Shall I sleep as soundly !
          Sleeping and Watching.

August 14

From the heavenly throned centre
   Heavenly voices shall repeat —
'Souls redeemed and pardoned, enter ; —
   For the chrism on you is sweet.'

          A Drama of Exile.

August 15

So I fell, struck down before her ! Do you
   blame me, friend, for weakness ?
'Twas my strength of passion slew me ! —
   fell before her like a stone ;
Fast the dreadful world rolled from me, on
   its roaring wheels of blackness !
When the light came I was lying in this
   chamber — and alone.
          Lady Geraldine's Courtship.

August 16

Oval cheeks encoloured faintly,
    Which a trail of golden hair
    Keeps from fading off to air;

And a forehead fair and saintly,
    Which two blue eyes undershine,
    Like meek prayers before a shrine.
                              A Portrait.

August 17

I am the nearest nightingale
That singeth in Eden after you;
And I am singing loud and true
And sweet,—I do not fail!

                    A Drama of Exile.

August 18

So, young muser, I sate listening
    To my Fancy's wildest word—
On a sudden, through the glistening
    Leaves around, a little stirred,
Came a sound, a sense of music, which was
    rather felt than heard.

                    The Lost Bower.

August 19

Thine angel glory sinks
  Down from me, down from me —
My beauty falls, methinks,
  Down from thee, down from thee !
    O my light-bearer,
    O my path-preparer,
  Gone from me, gone from me !
            A Drama of Exile.

August 20

Blessings on thee, dog of mine,
Pretty collars make thee fine,
  Sugared milk make fat thee !
Pleasures wag on in thy tail —
Hands of gentle motions fail
  Nevermore to pat thee !
          To Flush, My Dog.

August 21

Alas, the wretched children ! they are seeking
  Death in life, as best to have :
They are binding up their hearts away from
  breaking,
    With a cerement from the grave.
          The Cry of the Children.

August 22

Christ hath sent us down the angels ;
And the whole earth and the skies
Are illumed by altar-candles
Lit for blessed mysteries.
And a Priest's Hand, through creation,
Waveth calm and consecration —
  And Pan is dead.
        The Dead Pan.

August 23

Green the land is where my daily
    Steps in jocund childhood played —
Dimpled close with hill and valley,
    Dappled very close with shade !
Summer-snow of apple blossoms, running up
    from glade to glade.
        The Lost Bower.

August 24

' Yet God thee save, and may'st thou have
    A lady to thy mind,
More woman-proud and half as true
    As one thou leav'st behind !
And God me take with Him to dwell —
For Him I cannot love too well,
    As I have loved my kind.'
        The Romaunt of the Page.

August 25

'Tis aye a solemn thing to me
To look upon a babe that sleeps —
Wearing in its spirit-deeps
The unrevealèd mystery
Of its Adam's taint and woe,
Which, when they revealèd be,
Will not let it slumber so.

Isobel's Child.

August 26

Is the bower lost, then ?   Who sayeth
   That the bower indeed is lost?
Hark ! my spirit in it prayeth
   Through the solstice and the frost,—
And the prayer preserves it greenly to the
   last and uttermost.

The Lost Bower.

August 27

And thus, morning after morning, spite of
   oath, and spite of sorrow,
   Did I follow at her drawing, while the
   week-days passed along ;
Just to feed the swans this noontide, or to see
   the fawns to-morrow, —
   Or to teach the hill-side echo some sweet
   Tuscan in a song.

Lady Geraldine's Courtship.

August 28

What is true and just and honest,
What is lovely, what is pure —
All of praise that hath admonisht,—
All of virtue shall endure, —
These are themes for poets' uses,
Stirring nobler than the Muses—
          Ere Pan was dead.
          The Dead Pan.

August 29

    The essence of all beauty I call love.
The attribute, the evidence, and end,
The consummation to the inward sense,
Of beauty apprehended from without,
I still call love.

          A Drama of Exile.

August 30

They look up, with their pale and sunken
    faces,
    And their look is dread to see,
For you think you see their angels in their
    places,
    With eyes meant for Deity.
          The Cry of the Children.

August 31

Hold thy wrath,
Beloved Adam! let me answer him;
For this time he speaks truth, which we
should hear,
And asks for mercy, which I most should
grant,
In like wise, as he tells us — in like wise!
And therefore I thee pardon, Lucifer,
As freely as the streams of Eden flowed,
When we were happy by them.   So, depart.

A Drama of Exile.

September 1

Maker and High Priest,
I ask Thee not my joys to multiply, —
Only to make me worthier of the least.

Adequacy.

September 2

'What living man will bring a gift
Of his own heart, and help to lift
The tune? — The race is to the swift!'

So asked the angels.

A Vision of Poets.

September 3

If God compel thee to this destiny,
To die alone, with none beside thy bed
To ruffle round with sobs thy last word said,
And mark with tears the pulses ebb from
    thee —
Then pray alone, 'O Christ, come tenderly!'

The Thought of a Lonely Deathbed.

September 4

Quiet talk she liketh best,
  In a bower of gentle looks, —
  Watering flowers or reading books.

And her voice it murmurs lowly,
  As a silver stream may run,
  Which yet feels, you feel, the sun.

A Portrait.

September 5

Oh, shame to poet's lays
  Sung for the dole of praise, —
Hoarsely sung upon the highway
With that *obolum da mihi !*

A Lay of the Early Rose.

September 6

I dwell amid the city.
The great humanity which beats
Its life along the stony streets,
Like a strong unsunnèd river
In a self-made course, is ever
  Rolling on, rolling on !

The Soul's Travelling.

September 7

Tears! what are tears? The babe weeps in
    its cot,
The mother singing: at her marriage-bell,
The bride weeps: and before the oracle
Of high-faned hills, the poet hath forgot
That moisture on his cheeks.

Tears.

September 8

'I invite you, Mr. Bertram, to no hive for
    worldly speeches —
    Sir, I scarce should dare — but only where
    God asked the thrushes first:
And if *you* will sing beside them, in the covert
    of my beeches,
    I will thank you for the woodlands, — for
    the human world, at worst.'

Lady Geraldine's Courtship.

September 9

He is harmless — ye are sinful, —
    Ye are troubled — he, at ease!
From his slumber, virtue windful
    Floweth outward with increase —
Dare not bless him! but be blessed by his
    peace — and go in peace.

A Child Asleep.

September 10

As the moths around a taper,
   As the bees around a rose,
As in sunset, many a vapour, —
   So the spirits group and close
Round about a holy childhood, as if drinking
   its repose.

A Child Asleep.

September 11

Softly, softly ! make no noises !
   Now he lieth dead and dumb ;
Now he hears the angels' voices
   Folding silence in the room :
Now he muses deep the meaning of the
   Heaven-words as they come.

A Child Asleep.

September 12

Oh, of course, she charged her lacqueys to
   bear out the sickly burden,
   And to cast it from her scornful sight —
   but not *beyond* the gate —
She is too kind to be cruel, and too haughty
   not to pardon
Such a man as I — 'twere something to be
   level to her hate.

Lady Geraldine's Courtship.

September 13

' Or, oh, ye gifted givers ! ye
Who give your liberal hearts to me,
To make the world this harmony, —

' Are ye resigned that they be spent
To such world's help ? ' —

                  The Spirits bent
Their awful brows and said — ' Content ! '

          A Vision of Poets.

September 14

'Two words, indeed, of praying we remember;
  And at midnight's hour of harm, —
"Our Father," looking upward in the chamber
  We say softly for a charm.'

        The Cry of the Children.

September 15

The poet went out weeping, — and died
  abroad bereft there —
  The bird flew to his grave and died amid a
    thousand wails ! —
Yet, when I last came by the place, I swear
  the music left there
  Was only of the poet's song, and not the
    nightingale's !

        The Poet and the Bird.

September 16

' Drink,' said the lady, sad and slow —
' World's love behoveth thee to know.'
He looked to her, commanding so.

Her brow was troubled, but her eye
Struck clear to his soul. For all reply
He drank the water suddenly.

A Vision of Poets.

September 17

' Since thou shrivest my brother, fair mother,'
    said she,
'I count on thy priesthood for marrying of me!
And I know by the hills that the battle is
    done —
That my lover rides on — will be here with
    the sun,
        'Neath the eyes that behold thee !'
        The Lay of the Brown Rosary.

September 18

The poet went out weeping—the nightingale
    ceased chanting ;
  ' Now wherefore, O thou nightingale, is
    all thy sweetness done ?'
'I cannot sing my earthly things, the heavenly
    poet wanting,
  Whose highest harmony includes the lowest
    under sun.'
        The Poet and the Bird.

September 19

Touch not the harp to win the wreath:
Its tone is fame, its echo death!
The wreath may like the laurel grow,
Yet turns to cypress on the brow!
And as a flame springs clear and bright,
Yet leaveth ashes 'stead of light;
So genius (fatal gift!) is doomed
To leave the heart it fired, consumed.

To a Poet's Child.

September 20

A rose once grew within
A garden April-green,
In her loneness, in her loneness,
And the fairer for that oneness.

A Lay of the Early Rose.

September 21

Such innocence of action yet
Significance of object met
In his whole bearing strong and sweet.

A Vision of Poets.

September 22

Beautiful form of woman ! seeming made
Alone to shine in mirrors, there to braid
The hair and zone the waist — to garland
    flowers —
To walk like sunshine through the orange
    bowers —
To strike her land's guitar — and often see
In other eyes how lovely hers must be.
      The Deathbed of Teresa del Riego.

September 23

Then the good steed's rein she took, and his
    neck did kiss and stroke :
Soft he neighed to answer her, and then
    followed up the stair,
        For the love of her sweet look.

      Rhyme of the Duchess May.

September 24

Face and figure of a child, —
   Though too calm, you think, and tender,
   For the childhood you would lend her.

Yet child-simple, undefiled,
   Frank, obedient, — waiting still
   On the turnings of your will.
        A Portrait.

September 25

Down the sun dropt, large and red on the
　　towers of Linteged, —
Lance and spearhead on the height, bristling
　　strange in fiery light,
　　　　While the castle stood in shade.
　　　　　　　　Rhyme of the Duchess May.

September 26

Of all the thoughts of God that are
Borne inward unto souls afar,
Among the Psalmist's music deep,
Now tell me if there any is,
For gift or grace, surpassing this, —
　　' He giveth His belovèd sleep ? '
　　　　　　　　The Sleep.

September 27

　　　　　Henceforward, woman, rise
To thy peculiar and best altitudes
Of doing good and of enduring ill, —
Of comforting for ill, and teaching good,
And reconciling all that ill and good
Unto the patience of a constant hope, —
　　Rise with thy daughters !
　　　　　　　　A Drama of Exile.

Marry your pleasures

to your wo[rld]

And think life's

green well

worth its rose!

SONG.

September 28

And the air that waves the lilies waves this
   slender jet of water,
   Like a holy thought sent feebly up from
      soul of fasting saint!
Whereby lies a marble Silence, sleeping!
   (Lough the sculptor wrought her)
So asleep, she is forgetting to say *Hush!*—
   a fancy quaint.

Lady Geraldine's Courtship.

September 29

Some word she tried to say,
   Some *no* . . . ah, wellaway!
And the passion did o'ercome her,
But the fair frail leaves dropped from her.

A Lay of the Early Rose.

September 30

'He will kiss me on the mouth
Then and lead me as a lover,
   Through the clouds that praise his deeds;
   And, when soul-tied by one troth,
Unto *him* I will discover
   That swan's nest among the reeds.'

The Romance of the Swan's Nest.

October 1

'There is no God,' the foolish saith, —
  But none, 'There is no sorrow,'
And nature oft, the cry of faith,
  In bitter need will borrow.

The Cry of the Human.

October 2

There, Shakespeare! on whose forehead climb
The crowns o' the world! Oh, eyes sublime—
With tears and laughters for all time!

Here, Æschylus, — the women swooned
To see so awful when he frowned
As the gods did, — he standeth crowned.

A Vision of Poets.

October 3

Very copious are my praises,
  Though I sip it like a fly! —
Ah — but, sipping, — times and places
  Change before me suddenly —
As Ulysses' old libation
  Drew the ghosts from every part,
So your Cyprian wine, dear Græcian,
  Stirs the Hades of my heart.

Wine of Cyprus.

October 4

And that voice, I heard it pleading, for love's
    sake — for wealth, position, . . .
For the sake of liberal uses, and great
    actions to be done ; —
And she answered, answered gently — 'Nay,
    my lord, the old tradition
Of your Normans, by some worthier hand
    than mine is, should be won.'
          Lady Geraldine's Courtship.

October 5

This pedal strikes out in the air!
My instrument hath room to bear
Still fuller strains and perfecter.

        A Vision of Poets.

October 6

And well may the children weep before you;
    They are weary ere they run ;
They have never seen the sunshine, nor the
    glory
    Which is brighter than the sun :
They know the grief of men, but not the
    wisdom ;
They sink in the despair, without the calm.
        The Cry of the Children.

October 7

Ever, evermore the while in a slow silence
   she kept smiling, —
    While the shining tears ran faster down
    the blushing of her cheeks ;
Then with both her hands enfolding both of
   his, she softly told him,
    ' Bertram, if I say I love thee, . . . 'tis the
    vision only speaks.'

Lady Geraldine's Courtship.

October 8

O the little birds sang east, and the little
   birds sang west, —
And I smiled to think God's greatness flowed
   around our incompleteness, —
    Round our restlessness, His rest.

Rhyme of the Duchess May.

October 9

' I said, " My steed neighs in the court,
   My bark rocks on the brine,
And the warrior's vow, I am under now,
   To free the pilgrim's shrine :
But fetch the ring and fetch the priest,
   And call that daughter of thine,
And rule she wide, from my castle on Nyde,
   While I am in Palestine." '

The Romaunt of the Page.

October 10

'My page, my page, what grieves thee so,
 That the tears run down thy face?'—
'Alas, alas! mine own sister
 Was in thy lady's case!
But *she* laid down the silks she wore,
And followed him she wed before
Disguised as his true servitor,
 To the very battle-place.'

     The Romaunt of the Page.

October 11

Down she knelt at her lord's knee, and she
 looked up silently,—
And he kissed her twice and thrice, for that
 look within her eyes,
  Which he could not bear to see.

    Rhyme of the Duchess May.

October 12

'For myself I do not argue,' said I, 'though
 I love you, madam,—
But for better souls, that nearer to the
 height of yours have trod—
And this age shows, to my thinking, still
 more infidels to Adam,
Than directly, by profession, simple infidels
 to God.'

    Lady Geraldine's Courtship.

October 13

So oft the doing of God's will
Our foolish wills undoeth !
Yet softly breaks an idle dream
The morning light subdueth ;
And happier 'tis, to see the sun,
Than sleep, and dream a brighter one.

The Island.

October 14

'For life, so lovely-vain, —
For death, which breaks the chain, —
For this sense of present sweetness, —
And this yearning to completeness !'

A Lay of the Early Rose.

October 15

The woman singeth at her spinning-wheel
A pleasant chant, ballad, or barcarolle ;
She thinketh of her song, upon the whole,
Far more than of her flax ; and yet the reel
Is full, and artfully her fingers feel
With quick adjustment, provident control,
The lines, too subtly twisted to unroll,
Out to a perfect thread.

Work and Contemplation.

October 16

At dawn and at eve, mother, who sitteth there,
With the brown rosarie never used for a
    prayer?
Stoop low, mother, low! If we went there
    to see,
What an ugly great hole in that east wall
    must be
      At dawn and at even!
        The Lay of the Brown Rosary.

October 17

Day by day, with new desire,
    Toward my wood I ran in faith —
Under leaf and over brier —
    Through the thickets, out of breath —
Like the prince who rescued Beauty from the
    sleep as long as death.
        The Lost Bower.

October 18

There I read this ancient rhyme, while the
    bell did all the time
      Toll slowly.
And the solemn knell fell in with the tale of
    life and sin,
      Like a rhythmic fate sublime.
      Rhyme of the Duchess May.

October 19

In a child-abstraction lifted,
   Straightway from the bower I past;
Foot and soul being dimly drifted
   Through the greenwood, till, at last,
In the hill-top's open sunshine, I all con-
   sciously was cast.

The Lost Bower.

October 20

Learn to win a lady's faith
   Nobly, as the thing is high;
Bravely, as for life and death, —
   With a loyal gravity.

The Lady's 'Yes.'

October 21

'Drink,' said the lady, grave and slow,
'World's use behoveth thee to know.'
He drank the bitter wave below.

.   .   .   .

And as that solemn Dream withdrew,
The lady's kiss did fall anew
Cold on the poet's brow as dew.

A Vision of Poets.

October 22

Joy, most changeful of all things,
Flits away on rainbow wings;
And when they look the gayest, know,
It is that they are spread to go!

Song.

October 23

'Sword, thy noble use is done! — tower is
    lost, and shame begun : —
If we met them in the breach, hilt to hilt or
    speech to speech,
      We should die there, each for one.'

Rhyme of the Duchess May.

October 24

Choose me the loftiest cave of all,
    To make a place for prayer ;
And I will choose a praying voice
    To pour our spirits there.
How silverly the echoes run —
Thy will be done — Thy will be done!

The Island.

October 25

'But what if she mistook thy mind,
   And followed thee to strife ;
Then kneeling, did entreat thy love,
   As Paynims ask for life ? '
'I would forgive, and evermore
Would love her as my servitor,
   But little as my wife.'

The Romaunt of the Page.

October 26

A Harmony that finding vent,
Upward in grand ascension went,
Winged to a heavenly argument.

A Vision of Poets.

October 27

Eve. 'Twas an ill prayer: it shall be
   prayed no more ;
And God did use it for a foolishness,
Giving no answer.

A Drama of Exile.

October 28

Love's a virtue for heroes! — as white as the
   snow on high hills,
And immortal as every great soul is that
   struggles, endures and fulfils.

Lord Walter's Wife.

October 29

'Ah, that white hand!' he said quickly, —
   and in his he either drew it,
  Or attempted, for with gravity and instance
   she replied :
'Nay, indeed, my lord, this talk is vain, and
   we had best eschew it,
  And pass on, like friends, to other points
   less easy to decide.'

Lady Geraldine's Courtship.

October 30

And when betwixt the quick and dead the
   young fair Queen had vowed,
The living shouted, 'May she live! Victoria,
   live!' aloud —
And as the loyal shouts went up, true spirits
   prayed between,
'The blessings happy monarchs have be thine,
   O crownèd Queen!'

Crowned and Wedded.

October 31

Love us, God! love us, man! we believe, we
    achieve —
        Let us love, let us live,
        For the acts correspond —
        We are glorious — and DIE!
And again on the knee of a mild Mystery
        That smiles with a change,
        Here we lie!
        O DEATH, O BEYOND,
        Thou art sweet, thou art strange!

Life's Progress.

November 1

The dearest hands that clasp our hands, —
  Their presence may be o'er:
The dearest voice that meets our ear,
  That tone may come no more!
Youth fades; and then, the joys of youth,
  Which once refreshed our mind,
Shall come — as on those sighing woods,
  The chilling autumn wind.

The Autumn.

November 2

' She will weep her woman's tears, she will
    pray her woman's prayers, —
But her heart is young in pain, and her
    hopes will spring again
      By the suntime of her years.'

Rhyme of the Duchess May.

November 3

I think this nation's tears, thus poured together,
Nobler than shouts.   I think this funeral
Grander than crownings, though a Pope bless
    all!
I think this grave stronger than thrones! But
    whether
The crowned Napoleon or the buried clay
Be better, I discern not — Angels may.

Crowned and Buried.

November 4

On the east I sate that day, up against a
     willow grey : —
Through the rain of willow-branches, I could
     see the low hill-ranges,
          And the river on its way.

Rhyme of the Duchess May.

November 5

Meek leaves drop yearly from the forest-trees,
To show, above, the unwasted stars that pass
In their old glory.   O thou God of old,
Grant me some smaller grace than comes to
     these : —
But so much patience, as a blade of grass
Grows by, contented through the heat and
     cold.   *Patience taught by Nature.*

November 6

She has members in the Commons, she has
     lovers in the palace —
   And of all the fair court-ladies, few have
     jewels half as fine :
Even the prince has named her beauty,
     'twixt the red wine and the chalice :
   Oh, and what was *I* to love her? my
     beloved, my Geraldine !

Lady Geraldine's Courtship.

November 7

Future joy and far light
   Working such relations, —
Hear us singing gently —
   Exiled is not lost!
God, above the starlight,
   God above the patience,
Shall at last present ye
   Guerdons worth the cost.
           A Drama of Exile.

November 8

I will paint her as I see her,
   Ten times have the lilies blown
Since she looked upon the sun.

And her face is lily-clear,
   Lily-shaped, and dropped in duty
To the law of its own beauty.
           A Portrait.

November 9

He journeyed homeward through the wood,
And prayed along the solitude
Betwixt the pines, 'O God, my God!'

The golden morning's open flowings
Did sway the trees to murmurous bowings,
In metric chant of blessed poems.
           A Vision of Poets.

November 10

Mark how heavy white her eyelids! not a
 dream between them lingers!
And the left hand's index droppeth from
 the lips upon the cheek:
And the right hand, — with the symbol rose
 held slack within the fingers, —
Has fallen backward in the basin — yet
 this Silence will not speak!

Lady Geraldine's Courtship.

November 11

At last came silence. A slow kiss
Did crown his forehead after this;
His eyelids flew back for the bliss.

A Vision of Poets.

November 12

Then outlaughed the bridegroom, and out-
 laughed withal
Both maidens and youths, by the old chapel-
 wall—
'So she weareth no love-gift, kind brother,'
 quoth he,
'She may wear, an she listeth, a brown rosarie,
 Like a pure-hearted lady!'

The Lay of the Brown Rosary.

I have been in

the meadows

all the day,

And gathered

there.

the

nosegay

that you see;

Singing within myself as bird or bee.

IRREPARABLENESS.

November 13

'Each man clasp my hand, and swear, by the
    deed we failed in there, —
Not for vengeance, not for right, will ye
    strike one blow to-night!'
      Pale they stood around — to swear.

Rhyme of the Duchess May.

November 14

  Lucifer.   Ha, my clay-king!
Thou wilt not rule by wisdom very long
The after generations.   Earth, methinks,
Will disinherit thy philosophy
For a new doctrine suited to thine heirs;
Classing these present dogmas with the rest
Of the old-world traditions — Eden fruits
And saurian fossils.   *A Drama of Exile.*

November 15

Said he — 'I would dream so ever, like the
    flowing of that river,
  Flowing ever in a shadow, greenly onward
    to the sea;
So, thou vision of all sweetness — princely to
    a full completeness, —
  Would my heart and life flow onward —
    deathward, through this dream of THEE!'
      Lady Geraldine's Courtship.

November 16

'Though none us deign to bless,
  Blessèd are we, natheless;
Blessèd still, and consecrated
In that, rose, we were created.'

A Lay of the Early Rose.

November 17

The tramp of hoof, the flash of steel —
  The Paynims round her coming!
The sound and sight have made her calm, —
  False page, but truthful woman;
She stands amid them all unmoved;
A heart once broken by the loved
  Is strong to meet the foeman.

The Romaunt of the Page.

November 18

And if any poet knew her
  He would sing of her with falls
Used in lovely madrigals.

And if any painter drew her,
  He would paint her unaware
With a halo round the hair.

A Portrait.

November 19

Whatever's lost, it first was won :
We will not struggle nor impugn ;
Perhaps the cup was broken here,
That Heaven's new wine might show more
    clear.
I praise thee while my days go on.

                  De Profundis.

November 20

'Happy are all free peoples, too strong to be
    dispossessed ;
But blessed are those among nations who
    dare to be strong for the rest ! '

                  A Court Lady.

November 21

    ' And every moth and bee,
      Approach me reverently ;
Wheeling o'er me, wheeling o'er me,
Coronals of motioned glory.'

           A Lay of the Early Rose.

November 22

'What right have you, Madam, gazing in
  your shining mirror daily,
  Getting so, by heart, your beauty, which
  all others must adore, —
While you draw the golden ringlets down
  your fingers, to vow gaily, . . .
  You will wed no man that's only good to
  God, — and nothing more?'
  Lady Geraldine's Courtship.

November 23

And poor, proud Byron, sad as grave,
And salt as life ; forlornly brave,
And quivering with the dart he drave.

. . . .

His aimless thoughts in metre went
Like a babe's hand, without intent
Drawn down a seven-stringed instrument.
  A Vision of Poets.

November 24

As form, when colourless
Is nothing to the eye ; that pine-tree there,
Without its black and green, being all a blank,
So, without love, is beauty undiscerned
In man or angel.

  A Drama of Exile.

November 25

The young fawns are playing with the shadows;
   The young flowers are blowing toward the
     west ; —
But the young, young children, O my brothers,
   They are weeping bitterly ! —
They are weeping in the playtime of the others,
   In the country of the free.
        The Cry of the Children.

November 26

'For we throw out acclamations of self-
   thanking, self-admiring,
   With, at every mile run faster, — "O the
     wondrous, wondrous age,"
Little thinking if we work our souls as nobly
   as our iron,
Or if angels will commend us, at the goal
   of pilgrimage.'
        Lady Geraldine's Courtship.

November 27

My soul in love bounds forwarder,
   To meet the bounding waves !
Beside them is the home for me,
   Within the coral caves ; —
And near me two or three may dwell,
Whom dreams fantastic please as well.
        The Island.

November 28

In his vehement childhood he hurried within,
And knelt at her feet as in prayer against sin,
But a child at a prayer never sobbeth as he —
‘Oh, she sits with the nun of the brown rosary.
  At nights in the ruin !’

   The Lay of the Brown Rosary.

November 29

    Angel ! rather ask
What love is in thee, what love moves to thee,
And what collateral love moves on with thee;
Then shalt thou know if thou art beautiful.

    A Drama of Exile.

November 30

‘Oh, calm, below the marble grey,
 My father’s dust was strewn !
Oh, meek, above the marble grey,
 His image prayed alone !
The slanderer lied — the wretch was brave
For, looking up the minster-nave,
He saw my father’s knightly glaive
 Was changed from steel to stone.’
   The Romaunt of the Page.

December 1

I was so beautiful, so beautiful,
  My joy stood up within me bold and glad,
To answer God; and, when His work was
    full,
  To 'very good,' responded 'very glad!'
Filtered through roses did the light inclose me;
And bunches of the grape swang blue across
    me —
      Yet I wail!   *A Drama of Exile.*

December 2

Long live she! — send up loyal shouts — and
    true hearts pray between, —
'The blessings happy PEASANTS have be thine,
  O crownèd Queen!'

            Crowned and Wedded.

December 3

'Ye shall harness him aright, and lead upward
    to this height! —
Once in love and twice in war hath he borne
    me strong and far, —
      He shall bear me far to-night.'
      Rhyme of the Duchess May.

December 4

' His organ's pedals strike along
These poets' hearts, which metal-strong
They gave him without count of wrong—

' From which foundation he can guide
Up to God's feet, from these who died,
An anthem fully glorified ! '

A Vision of Poets.

December 5

Oh, she fluttered like a tame bird, in among
    its forest-brothers,
    Far too strong for it; then drooping, bowed
      her face upon her hands;
And I spake out wildly, fiercely, brutal truths
    of her and others :
    I, she planted in the desert, swathed her,
      windlike, with my sands.

Lady Geraldine's Courtship.

December 6

' I know by the hills,' she resumed, calm and
    clear,
' By the beauty upon them, that *He* is anear !
Did they ever look *so* since he bade me adieu ?
Oh, love in the waking, sweet brother, is true
    As St. Agnes in sleeping.'

The Lay of the Brown Rosary.

December 7

'What bell will yield a tone,
  Swung in the air alone?
If no brazen clapper bringing,
Who can hear the chimed ringing?'

A Lay of the Early Rose.

December 8

'Where is thy master, scornful page,
  That we may slay or bind him?'—
'Now search the lea, and search the wood,
  And see if ye can find him!
Nathless, as hath been often tried,
Your Paynim heroes faster ride
  Before him than behind him.'

The Romaunt of the Page.

December 9

And the tender bride-mother breaks off una-
  ware
From an Ave, to think that her daughter is
  fair,—
Till in nearing the chapel, and glancing before,
She seeth her little son stand at the door,—
  Is it play that he seeketh?

The Lay of the Brown Rosary.

December 10

My future will not copy fair my past
On any leaf but Heaven's.   Be fully done,
Supernal Will !   I would not fain be one
Who, satisfying thirst and breaking fast
Upon the fulness of the heart, at last
Saith no grace after meat.

Past and Future.

December 11

In the pleasant orchard closes,
   ' God bless all our gains,' say we ;
But ' May God bless all our losses,'
   Better suits with our degree. —
Listen, gentle — ay, and simple ! Listen, chil-
dren on the knee !

The Lost Bower.

December 12

Slowly and thankfully
   The young page bowed his head :
His large eyes seemed to muse a smile,
   Until he blushed instead ;
And no lady in her bower pardiè,
   Could blush more sudden red —
' Sir Knight, — thy lady's bower to me
   Is suited well,' he said.

The Romaunt of the Page.

December 13

By your truth she shall be true,
    Ever true, as wives of yore ;
And her *Yes*, once said to you,
    SHALL be Yes for evermore.

The Lady's 'Yes.'

December 14

How he sleepeth ! having drunken
    Weary childhood's mandragore,
From his pretty eyes have sunken
    Pleasures, to make room for more —
Sleeping near the withered nosegay, which he
    pulled the day before.

A Child Asleep.

December 15

'Herein is room, and shall be room
While Time lasts, for new hearts to come
Consummating while they consume.

A Vision of Poets.

December 16

I praise thee while my days go on;
I love thee while my days go on;
Through dark and dearth, through fire and
    frost,
With emptied arms and treasure lost,
I thank thee while my days go on.

De Profundis.

December 17

What are we set on earth for? Say, to toil —
Nor seek to leave thy tending of the vines,
For all the heat o' the day, till it declines,
And Death's mild curfew shall from work
    assoil.
God did anoint thee with His odorous oil,
To wrestle, not to reign.

Work.

December 18

Exiled human creatures,
    Let your hope grow larger!
Larger grows the vision
    Of the new delight.
From this chain of Nature's,
    God is the Discharger;
And the Actual's prison
    Opens to your sight.

A Drama of Exile.

December 19

Full upon his she turned her face, —
'What, ho, sir poet! dost thou pace
Our woods at night, in ghostly chase

'Of some fair Dryad of old tales,
Who chaunts between the nightingales,
And over sleep by song prevails?'
A Vision of Poets.

December 20

Who meet there, my mother, at dawn and at
 even?
Who meet by that wall, never looking to
 Heaven?
O sweetest my sister, what doeth with *thee*
The ghost of a nun with a brown rosarie,
  And a face turned from Heaven?
  The Lay of the Brown Rosary.

December 21

'Onora, Onora' — her mother is calling —
She sits at the lattice and hears the dew fall-
 ing
Drop after drop from the sycamores laden
With dew as with blossom — and calls home
 the maiden —
  'Night cometh, Onora.'
  The Lay of the Brown Rosary.

December 22

I count the dismal time by months and years,
Since last I felt the green sward under foot,
And the great breath of all things summer-
     mute
Met mine upon my lips.   Now earth appears
As strange to me as dreams of distant spheres.

The Prisoner.

December 23

'But a woman's will dies hard, in the hall or
     on the sward !
By that grave, my lords, which made me
     orphaned girl and dowered lady,
          I deny you wife and ward.'

Rhyme of the Duchess May.

December 24

Lucretius — nobler than his mood !
Who dropped his plummet down the broad
Deep universe, and said ' No God,'

Finding no bottom ! he denied
Divinely the divine, and died
Chief poet on the Tiber-side.

A Vision of Poets.

December 25

Art Thou a King, then?
     Come, His universe,
  Come, crown me Him a King!
Pluck rays from all such stars as never fling
     Their light where fell a curse,
And make a crowning for this kingly brow!
     The Virgin Mary to the Child Jesus.

December 26

Beloved! it is not good to speak with him.
Go from us, Lucifer, and speak no more:
We have no pardon which thou dost not
     scorn,
Nor any bliss, thou seest, for coveting,
Nor innocence for staining.   Being bereft,
We would be alone, — Go!
               A Drama of Exile.

December 27

When I attain to utter forth in verse
Some inward thought, my soul throbs audibly
Along my pulses, yearning to be free,
And something farther, fuller, higher, rehearse,
To the individual, true, and the universe,
In consummation of right harmony!

               Insufficiency.

December 28

'So works this music on the earth!
God so admits it, sends it forth,
To add another worth to worth.'

A Vision of Poets.

December 29

'Three larks shall leave a cloud;
To my whiter beauty vowed —
Singing gladly all the moontide, —
Never waiting for the suntide.'

A Lay of the Early Rose.

December 30

And ye lifted up your head, and it seemed as
    if He said,
    'My Beloved, is it so?
    Have ye tasted of my woe? —
    Of my Heaven ye shall not fail!'

The Fourfold Aspect.

December 31

Light human nature is too lightly tost
And ruffled without cause; complaining on,
Restless with rest — until, being overthrown,
It learneth to lie quiet.

Discontent.